Baby Ti...
for new daas

Baby's
First Year

Dedication

This book is dedicated to husbands because
I believe all men should be prepared
for what they are in for after delivery . . .
by the way, I'm not talking about the baby.

Baby Tips™
for new dads

Baby's
First Year

JEANNE MURPHY

FISHER
BOOKS

Publishers: Bill Fisher
Helen V. Fisher
Howard W. Fisher

Managing Editor: Sarah Trotta

Cover Design: FifthStreet*design*, Berkeley, CA

Production: Deanie Wood
Randy Schultz
Josh Young

Cover Illustration: © 1998 Sharon Howard Constant

Illustrations: Cathie Lowmiller

Published by
Fisher Books
4239 W. Ina Road, Suite 101
Tucson, Arizona 85741
(520) 744-6110

To pass along your own helpful suggestions to
new mothers for future editions of this book,
please call (800) 617-4603.

Library of Congress Cataloging-in-Publication Data
Murphy, Jeanne, 1964-
    [Baby tips for new dads, baby's first year]
    Jeanne Murphy's baby tips for new dads,
       baby's first year.
       p.   cm.
    Includes index.
    ISBN 1-55561-169-9
    1. Infants. 2. Husbands. 3. Fathers.
    HQ774.M887 1998
    649'. 122—dc21   98-16466
                                                 CIP

Notice: The information in this book is true and complete to the best of our knowledge. It is offered with no guarantees on the part of the author or Fisher Books. Author and publisher disclaim all liability in connection with the use of this book.

The suggestions made in this book are opinions and are not meant to supersede a doctor's recommendation in any way. Always consult your doctor before beginning any new program.

Contents

 Introduction

Congratulations on the birth of your baby! Fatherhood is a rewarding experience and I'm sure you will be great at it.

You will probably find parenting easy, because adjusting to your baby is nothing compared to the changes you and your wife will experience! Here are some experience-tested thoughts and suggestions from my husband and me to help you through this adjustment.

Most important, stick together! Use humor whenever you start to feel tense. Smiling releases hormones that can dramatically reduce stress. I especially hope this book helps in that department!

Best wishes to you and your family!

To fellow dads:

Once you've been around the block, you refer to the postpartum period as "boot-ie camp."

That's because you really need to have some type of survival training in order to live through it.

I salute you!

Mr. Jan J. Murphy

Hormones and How to Handle Them

If you find your wife with beads of perspiration on her forehead and she says, "It's sweat! It is caused by **HARD WORK,** and it is spelled **S-T-R-E-S-S**," you are talking to a gigantic, postpartum, hot-flash hormone, not your wife. . . . **Run for it!**

The term "postpartum" is synonymous with PMS . . . **parental-mental syndrome.**

Yes—technically your wife does have some of the same characteristics as a crazy person during the postpartum period. But it's only **temporary** insanity.

If your wife suddenly decides to cut her hair, change the furniture, paint the walls or buy a new car, ask her to sleep on it. After having a baby, women's attitudes about all sorts of things fluctuate wildly. If you encourage your wife to sleep on it, probably she will have changed her mind completely by morning.

If you come home for lunch or dinner and your wife's hair is wet, her face is pale and her robe is still on, don't ask if she's sick.

My father has five kids, and he tells me to tell you this: "Sometimes it's better to punt on the third down . . . especially when your wife is a new mother."

He said all men would know what he means.

Remember, the main ingredients for a time bomb are:

1 part postpartum hormones

2 parts champagne or red wine

For tear gas, stir in a few emotional statements.

Unless you are trying to pick a fight, don't even think about taking up golf lessons or starting any other new hobbies right now. God has just given you a new hobby and you'll be great at it after a little practice.

Never, never, never
wake up the baby!

Play around on the floor and be spontaneous with **everyone** in your family, including your wife.

Remember: In the back of your wife's mind, she is probably thinking, "One baby is enough," so don't act like a baby yourself right now.
(By the way, only **she** is allowed this particular thought.)

Destroy the snooze button on your alarm clock as a goodwill gesture. All your wife needs is the baby **and** a radio waking her up every ten minutes. The best way to avoid having a highly irritable, frustrated, overworked, underpaid, sleep-deprived wife is for you just to get up and go to work after the first buzz.

Don't tip over the baby's bottles if they are upside-down, drying on the counter, and don't open the dryer and remove just your own clean shirt—unless you are looking for some serious retaliation. I am not **suggesting** retaliation—it's just that this response becomes natural for women once they have a child. It's actually more instinctive than motherhood for many women.

If your wife says, "I need to get out of here," say, "Do you want me to come with you, or should I stay at home with our beautiful child? Because I could go either way."

I remember having an argument with my husband only four days after the baby was born. I don't remember what the fight was about, but I do remember that, although I was mad, I was also elated that I had lost nearly 28 pounds in just four days! In retrospect, I think the argument may have been my

Baby Tips

fault, because you can't behave normally with that type of weight loss and hormonal fluctuation. It was a significant day for me, and I think I need to apologize to my husband for it. (I'm sorry, honey. I really do love you . . . and you are a great father. You're so natural at it!)

Let your wife hear you sing a lullaby to your baby.

In case you were wondering . . . "no" means "yes" and "yes" means "no."

Don't develop a case of postpartum blues. That is **really** annoying. New mothers share everything with their new babies. It is an all-consuming, exhausting experience and we are not used to it. We do not want to have to cheer up our husbands in addition. Besides, postpartum blues is **our** problem and we deserve to have it to ourselves!

If your wife describes something that is bothering her and asks you how you feel about it, agree with her in a sympathetic way, at least for the moment.

If your wife's hair starts looking dull and some falls out, don't tell her about it. Your best bet is to pretend you don't notice.

If she was up all night with the baby and you didn't help, back-pedal! Leave a note on the table that says something like this:

"I'm sorry you had such a bad night last night. When I looked in on you, you were sleeping in the chair and I didn't want to wake you. I love you and I am so proud of you for being such a good mother."

Thank your wife for having your child. After all, nobody else could have done it so well for you.

Get yourself an imaginary surfboard and expect at any moment to hop on and ride an emotional tidal wave. (Remember, I said **imaginary** surfboard.)

Women love it when men say things like, "I feel so bad for you. I just wish I could help more."

Baby Tips

Whenever your wife says she needs a baby-sitter, say, "Absolutely! I don't know how you do without one. You do so much. At $3.50 an hour, baby-sitters are a real bargain."

If you think you can't win, you're right.

Baby Tips

Hug your wife twice a day! (This will disarm her completely.)

Babies love guys who look them straight in the eye when they are talking to them . . . and so do wives.

If your wife is soaking wet and doesn't seem to realize it, she was either peed on, puked on, she's having a hormonal surge or she got out of the shower and forgot to dry off because the baby was crying. Get her a towel.

Take up tennis lessons with your wife. Not only is it great exercise, but you can spend quality time alone together . . . or take out your aggressions on one another!

Don't eat or drink the last of anything in the refrigerator or pantry ever again unless you want to starve to death. If your wife looks for it and it's gone, she will make a point of not replacing it.

If you have already told your wife, "It doesn't matter what you do, you are always beautiful and you always amaze me," you can throw this book away. You don't need it.

The Monumentally Sensitive Issue of Weight

Some mothers have a distorted conception of how they look physically because their weight fluctuation over the course of nine months was so tremendous. So, if your wife says, "Do you like this dress?" always say, "Oh, yes!" unless you are a graduate of the Fashion Institute of Technology or a licensed psychologist.

Unless your wife has an exceptional sense of humor, don't laugh while she is putting on lingerie.

Don't suddenly start talking about your own weight-loss goals in front of your wife. And don't surprise her with exercise equipment for the house unless she asks for it.

If you give your wife new clothes, buy clothes at least two sizes bigger than her usual size. Then cut off the size tag and act stupid. (We women do this to our men all the time.)

Don't buy your wife a sexy nightie until you know the time is right.

If you want to give your wife chocolates, send them from a "secret admirer." If she eats the whole box and then feels fat, she can't blame you. You can say you had nothing to do with them. (I say, stick with flowers!)

Ask your wife if she wants you to call her "momma" **before** you try it.

If your wife says she feels fat, say, "Honey, you just had a baby." (But sound compassionate—otherwise you're dead.)

Most important, only talk about OTHER mothers who are fat.

What to Do and Say

Make sure to use the expression, "I still can't believe what a natural you are at this!" every time you introduce the subject of mothering or parenthood to your wife.

It's better to give your wife a reason to say "thank you" than it is for you to find a way to say "I'm sorry."

When you said, "I do," did you read the fine print at the bottom of the marriage license? Basically, "I do" is superseded by the expression "I will" once there are children.

It applies to things like making the bed, cleaning the bathrooms, washing the dishes, cleaning the house, mowing the

Baby Tips

lawn, shopping for groceries, feeding the dog, picking up the dry cleaning, taking care of birthday gifts for your in-laws, etc.

When everything is going really well, offer to take care of the baby because your wife will say, "No thanks" —but she'll love you for asking.

Face it, by the time you learn how to fix the plumbing, your kids will have graduated from college, so just call a professional. As a new father, you have a more important job waiting: Mothers need fathers to baby-sit while they grocery shop and do some other really important stuff. So hurry up and finish whatever it is you're doing so she can get some real work done!

Try to encourage friendships with other parents. New moms want to be around people with experience.

Baby Tips

Insider tip: If you are going to a family gathering on Sunday, let your wife sleep well on Saturday night. She will be in a great mood for the party and everyone will think you are a saint.

Tell your wife every day "I don't know how you do it," and you will be way ahead of the game.

Use the same expression, something like "Uh-oh!", every time you see your baby. She will begin to bond with you and look to you the way she looks to her mother. This is a wonderful experience . . . especially for mom!

If you are in a stand-off situation with your wife, suggest one of her relatives serve as godparent.

Always use the words "we should," not "you should."

Buy a remote-controlled starting device for your wife's car (not yours).

Remind each other to stop and smell the roses, because this is really a very short, special time. You will be back to normal in a few months . . . NOT.

Treat your wife to a spa day and a massage. (But don't forget to plan ahead for a baby-sitter as well, because otherwise your nice gesture will turn into a nightmare.)

If you have a special memory of childhood, such as going to parades, camping, boating or going to the beach with your parents, make it a priority to pass the same joy to your child. (Your wife will enjoy it too.)

If you take your wife out to dinner and she starts to bring up the baby and all the stress she's under, put your finger across her lips and gently whisper, "Not tonight. You've been working so hard! This night is just for you. Let's relax and have a good time."

Establish holiday traditions with your child, such as reading *Over the River and through the Wood*, a poem about the joys of a Thanksgiving visit to Grandmother's house. It was written by a woman named Lydia Maria Francis Child in the 1800s and can be found in several editions at your local library.

If your wife makes a suggestion, respond first by saying something positive about it. Propose improvements after that point.

Spoil your wife now. Your baby has plenty of time to be spoiled later.

Set up charge accounts at your local pizza parlor and Chinese take-out restaurant. This step will make meals on hectic days much easier. As a matter of fact, set up charge-card accounts everywhere—like everyone else with kids does.

When the going gets tough, whisk your wife away overnight! (Just don't respond by becoming a tough guy, because mothers need all the sensitivity they can get.)

Keep the peace and change a diaper now and then. Offer to pick up dinner (or cook it) without being asked.

If you are trying to make your wife feel better but you say things such as, "If you really want the house to be tidier, maybe you should get up earlier to clean it," find a rehab center and admit yourself as an inpatient. You need **at least** 30 days of treatment to correct the warped psychology you are using with your wife.

Be a hero and GENTLY turn off the monitor one night when your wife finally falls asleep. Then take care of the baby yourself.

If any of her family members are around, make absolutely certain you are the one who is carrying the diaper bag and pushing the stroller.

You know your wife's limits better than she does, so don't let her take on more than she can handle. Even though Lamaze classes are over, you're still the team coach—now more than ever.

Surprise your wife and hire a house-cleaner to clean your home, either while your wife is in the hospital or the day after she gets home. (Whoever you hire must be inexpensive, old and not expect much conversation as she power-cleans!)

If you have anything really important to say to your wife about the way she mothers, but the baby is OK, **keep it to yourself.**

Humanitarian Albert Schweitzer once said, "Example is not the main thing in influencing others, it is the only thing."

What Absolutely
NOT to Do or Say

Rule #1: Don't be a better "mother" than your wife, even if you are.

Baby Tips

NEVER use the expression, "I'm so tired"—but especially not the day after the baby is born.

Remember, your goal right now is to minimize your wife's many new responsibilities, not add to them. With that in mind, don't bring home a new pet "for the baby."

Never go to a family party if you are in a bad mood. You will be eaten alive by her relatives.

If you have something to say to your wife, speak up! Don't say it to the baby, hoping your wife will overhear it.

Don't roll over and put a pillow over your head when you hear the baby start to scream through the baby monitor. It is better to deal with a crying baby than to handle a mother in full scream.

Don't sleep in and believe you won't hear about it.

You can take naps . . . but only when the baby is napping, too.

Baby Tips

It's common for a new baby to take several weeks to bond with his father, so hang in there! Most important, don't mope around the house regretting it if you didn't talk to the baby when it was in the womb because that's **really irritating.**

Don't be a grump! Imagine life without baby monitors, VCRs and disposable diapers. (You should be feeling better already.)

If you expect praise just because you are a father, you're probably also expecting a bonus this year just because you show up at work.

Don't make your tone of voice deeper, to sound like a Dennis-the-Menace dad, the minute you become a father. It's annoying.

Don't volunteer for overtime at work unless you discuss it with your wife in advance. No matter how much you may be helping the family's bottom line, it won't go over well if you tell your wife the good news when she's having a bad day.

Do what you say you will do. Don't offer to baby-sit so your wife can have an evening out and then hire a baby-sitter so you can leave, too.

Try not to say things that are obvious, such as, "Tell me again, how do you know when the diaper needs to be changed?"

Never say: "Hey, you delivered the baby early! Can I go to the football game Sunday?"

If you've invited your wife on a date, don't rent a movie. You will be stood up. Your wife will admit without hesitation that she would rather sleep than watch a movie at home on "date night." Avoid rejection and think of something completely different you can do together, like bowling or seeing a play at your local high school or university.

Under no circumstances use the expression, "So, did you do anything today?" unless you want to be told off.

Never answer a question with the question, "How should I know?"

Don't say things to the baby like, "Mommy is going to give you a bath when she is done cooking dinner, so don't fall asleep yet"—unless you want to take a bath in your dinner.

Don't correct your wife's child-rearing practices unless you know she is absolutely, positively, unequivocally wrong. This may include getting the proof in writing, signed by her mother. Remember, our parenting examples were our parents, so we all have slightly different approaches.

Unless you are willing to take them on yourself, don't suggest new projects.

Other General Survival Tips

Basically, change completely forever.

The declaration "I'll be back in five minutes" is heard by your wife as "I am indefinitely unavailable and preoccupied with my own business."

It's never really 50/50 between you and your wife. It's 100/100.

Unless your wife is a taxi driver, bus driver or race-car driver, "helping with meaningful tasks around the home" does **not** include changing the oil in the car.

The first thing you give your child is your name, so make him proud of it.

If you have a daughter, people will terrorize you with stories about wedding costs. If you have a son, they will taunt you with comments about how people are beginning to share wedding costs.

By the way, "helping out with meaningful tasks around the home" is a broad expression but it includes grocery shopping, picking up the dry-cleaning, handling the finances and interviewing for the part-time job your wife will want you to get when she decides to stay home with the baby.

Your baby has a small body and big ears . . . but she's really cute!

Your baby records everything you do and say. He will become more like you than your wife will over the years to come.

If you can't find anyone you can relate to about your wife, have a heart-to-heart with your baby. Your baby has been around the block and knows exactly how to get what she wants from her.

The best dads in the world have reputations for alternating pick-ups and drop-offs with their wives if their baby goes to day care.

Does the statement, "Don't stop at the grocery store without calling first!" sound familiar? Just do it.

After a few weeks you'll get used to the smell of a diaper pail in your home. You won't even notice it. (Think of it as a different kind of litter box. People with cats know what I'm talking about.)

Start getting used to burping and passed gas.

I'm not talking about the baby.

Children become their parents, so do what you can now to help them become great parents later.

Remove the words "happy hour," "office party," "office gathering" or anything vaguely resembling those terms from your vocabulary.

Everyone else may be having happy hour between 5:00 p.m. and 7:30 p.m., but you will be having "cranky hour." (Don't worry, it doesn't last forever.)

If anyone offers you advice on parenting, say, "Thanks. I was just getting ready to ask about that."

Insider Tip: If you get the laundry folded and the diaper changed within 15 minutes of your wife's return from shopping, you will continue to be happily married.

If it seems as though your wife does it all, she does! (A true comment from a real husband and father.)

It may have been OK to be lost and drive around for hours before you had a baby. But now you have a restless child in a rear-facing restraint system, and it's going to be **your** rear facing the street unless you know exactly how to get where you are going **before** you pack up the family in the car!

Getting adjusted to parenthood is not always a fun and happy experience. As long as you like the baby, you are normal!

The instant your child is born, your perspective on life changes completely. Things you never thought much about before, like Father's Day, become the center of your universe.

The expression "afternoon delight" now means the husband comes home during the lunch hour to baby-sit while his wife takes a nap.

Before the baby, if you kicked your wife's foot under the table during a party conversation, she would have politely changed the subject. Now she's a mother, there's little time for sugarcoating. So be prepared: She might surprise you with the public announcement, "Stop kicking my foot! . . . and what do you want, anyway?"

Before the baby, it may have been OK to be a procrastinator, but now, **all bets are off.**

"The grass is always greener on the other side of the fence." On closer inspection, you usually find the people living there have a lawn-maintenance service, but the interior of their house is a mess.

Don't bother to compare your child or family to other families—you just never know all the circumstances.

Baby Tips

Being a good dad and husband isn't the result of a gene. It's the result of commitment.

Make a commitment to clean up after your wife and child (or children). And smile while you're at it!

The best way to insure marital peace is to use baby-sitters who are not related to either of you.

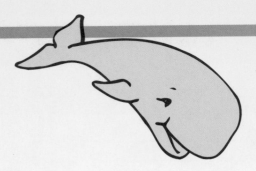

People with children are usually painfully honest, annoying and right.

*B*e realistic about your new lifestyle, and you and your wife will get along fine. The days of neatly pressed pants and shirts are over.

While you're at it, expect your pockets to be filled with cereal and small toys from now on, instead of money.

Consider buying a home this year if you haven't already. This way you get a tax deduction from the baby **and** from the mortgage interest, so the move could be advantageous.

Index

Look for These Baby Tips™ Books
& Other Fine Fisher Books Titles